GHOST RIVER

Kris Johnson grew up in America's Puget Sound basin, flanked by the Olympic Mountains and the North Cascades. She moved to the UK in her early twenties, living in various parts of England and Scotland before completing her PhD in Creative Writing, exploring the relationship between deep ecology and contemporary western American literature, at Newcastle University. She is the recipient of a DYCP grant from Arts Council England, and has published her work in journals including *The Poetry Review*, *Poetry Ireland Review*, *Poetry London* and *Poetry Northwest*. Her debut pamphlet, *Skinny Dip*, was published in 2022 by Enchiridion. Her first book-length collection, *Ghost River*, was published by Bloodaxe in 2023.

KRIS JOHNSON

Ghost River

BLOODAXE BOOKS

ISBN: 978 1 78037 647 9

First published 2023 by
Bloodaxe Books Ltd,
Eastburn,
South Park,
Hexham,
Northumberland NE46 1BS

www.bloodaxebooks.com
For further information about Bloodaxe titles
please visit our website and join our mailing list
or write to the above address for a catalogue.

Supported using public funding by
**ARTS COUNCIL
ENGLAND**

Cover design: Neil Astley & Pamela Robertson-Pearce.

Digital reprint of the 2023 Bloodaxe Books edition.

for my family

ACKNOWLEDGEMENTS

Acknowledgements are due to the editors of the following publications where some of these poems, or versions of them, first appeared: *Ambit*, *Butcher's Dog*, *The Irish Literary Review*, *Poem*, *Poetics of the Archive* (NCLA), *Poetry Ireland Review*, *Poetry London*, *Poetry Northwest*, *The Poetry Review*, *Poetry Salzburg Review* and *The Rialto*. Thanks also to the editors of Enchiridion for publishing my pamphlet, *Skinny Dip*, where some of these poems first appeared.

My sincere thanks to Sean O'Brien for his mentorship and for supporting the development of this body of work; to Gerry Wardle and the members of The Northern Poetry Workshop; to Nadine Boughton, Joanne Cornwell and Wendy Heath; and to Hannah Lowe, David Spittle and Thomas Brush. I am also grateful to Neil Astley and everyone at Bloodaxe Books for bringing this collection into the world.

To my family, thank you for believing that writing was a good path. To John Challis, my poetry confidant, my deepest gratitude is reserved for you. Thank you for all you have done to ensure these poems and this collection exist.

CONTENTS

Rainier

I am in love with this mountain
that all summer long threatens to kill

my father. Swallow him in the pale blue
Emmons, crush him beneath an avalanche

or send him sliding down the Kautz –
his crampons failing on pre-dawn ice.

This mountain I love will one day knock
on the door of my mother's home,

unearth the graves of my relatives
and carry hyacinths and coffins

down the Duwamish, out into the Sound.

Bodies of Water

At night, when I am caught
in the near-dark and I hear
the neighbours arguing
I also smell the tar of the pier,
skid row, exhaust
from the viaduct.

Green water blooms
with jellyfish
and bright anemones.
I am trying to remember
the kelp forests,
but I am not here

because I am on the ferry.
The distance does not erase
the land we've left
but makes it visible: hills
that rise beyond hills, tiers of houses,
the shoreline unwound.

If I were to name the water
I look across? But I'm not interested
in names as the sun dips
behind the islands.
I am breaking-in my boots
and thinking of pain and air and ice.

My father guides me over
the mouth of the crevasse
and I wonder if my mother
felt robbed of the sky
when he left. From the summit,
the land beneath me is a map.

This is the world: some friend's
parent's minivan, a fat stretch of I-5,
summer heat in the parking lot,
the cold descent
into skunk cabbage bogs
followed by that driftwood tang.

I sleepwalk into rivers
over-spilling their banks,
white foam rising
from the falls, a silver-lit ocean
where my grandfather
scatters ash.

Lake Americana

Idle boats, gasoline, music
poured over still water
and somewhere in the distance
an industrial lawn mower churning
goose shit into chlorophyllic pulp.
Cannon ball, somersault, vodka
mixed with Orange Crush.
Already I plan what I will warn
my daughter of: duck itch, algal blooms,
any dare that has her swim
beneath the dock.
Lakes being one road
to many deaths, I will tell her
to stay where I can see her,
that it is not true the lake will hold you
till you remember how to pray.
No one has ever seen the boy
vault feet first from the water,
his body a sickle that lands silently
on the pier dry and breathing.

Skinny Dip

I do not let my mother's warnings,
curfews or those beautiful boys
drowned earlier in the summer
(drugs, a dare failed, cracked skull,
broken neck) when the lake
was high and cold stop me.

Floating in the black, I imagine
their unrecovered bodies
rising beneath me, pressing my hips
level with the surface of the water;
my navel, nipples, eyes and lips
aligned with the constellations

above me. In ripples
and waves I hear them whisper
my name and feel their tongues,
strong from great mouthfuls
of water, licking my neck,
my shoulders, the soles of my feet.

The Desiccation

I once loved a wet man.
From his lips I drank the Pacific,
Fragrance Lake trout-green and shallow.
I followed him the weeping months
licking dew from devil's club,
nettle, bracken fern, sequoia.
He promised to baptise me
in the Salish Sea. With him
I would never thirst.

But Father, haunted by clouds
and distrustful of those tides
loyal to the moon, complained
I'd grown heavy as a wave.
He warned of the salmon scales
that would stud my tongue,
of the gills I'd grow, the chill
I would suffer. He said
my hands would turn to fins.

Beneath bare cattle country sky
we drove east to where water
is contained in rivers.
Land of rattlesnakes and sagebrush;
mesas that crack into gorges,
their wide jaws toothed with basalt.
There he tied me: my skin
to lizard, heart to blaze, body
to be purified by sun.

From me he drained
the sluice of the Duwamish,
Nooksack, Skagit, Green – gave thanks

as rain and ocean left my pores.
Now my legs are thin as a raven's,
my hair coarse as a coyote's pelt.
I no longer thirst but burn
and flick my tongue to the Palouse wind,
crying *Father, I am cured.*
I am saved.

Yellow Jackets

We are after the same thing,
the yellow jackets and me, who peels
back the pear's skin to suckle.

Half-fill a five-gallon bucket with water,
fold raw bacon over a string, secure above water.
My grandmother's instructions for setting a trap.
What she knew had been learned by pain.

Summer is good to us here: pears,
yellow plums, the north shore
with salmon berries and blackcaps.
All across town zucchinis and corn ripen.

I could live forever this way – the sound
of fruit loosening from the trees,
the yellow jackets falling, fat and stunned.

What I meant when I said goodnight

Stay until the bats retire and, drunk on stars,
the moon trips over the horizon; until Orion
unbuckles his belt, our skin solves the equation
for dew point and the owl splits the night into whispers;
until we have read every black knot on the birch,
written poems to lichen, shared bark with deer
and against our nails they've scratched their velvet;
until we are fluent in conifer, seeds mistake
our legs for logs, moss grows from our pores
and crows sleep on our shoulders.

The Doe

I

Five minutes into my run,
I come across the doe.

She doesn't struggle as I slide
down the bank to kneel

beside her in the blackberry
and last autumn's alder.

I stroke her white muzzle and neck.
There, there. There, there.

As morning drones and the sun
begins to lift the frost, I rise –

stagger home on feet numbed
and blunt as hooves.

I try to wash her from me,
but the steam of her swift breathing

fills the bathroom. I wear her scent
on my wrists, the touch of fur a secret.

II

Because once I swerved
to miss a buck on this road,
the doe is on my mind
as we slow to greet taillights
and a shower of glass
across the highway.

Diners from the café shiver
on the kerb, the chef
conducts traffic and a man
with a face of stone
looms over the body
of a motorcyclist.
How small it seems
as they pull
a Pendleton blanket
head to toe.

I know the radio plays,
know sirens blare
as we let police cars pass,
but the only sound I hear
is my voice: how I tried

to comfort her
the way I remembered
and wanted my mother's touch.
I hear me tell you
of her animal warmth,
how I longed to lay beside her
the way I used to press against you
in the minutes before sleep.

Nisqually Delta Blue

It's the house that's got us down. Not that it isn't
beautiful on its solitary peninsula, no sign of an access
road through the tree-lined ridge that descends to the
water. It's the whole place. We could never afford it.
Not the mortgage, not the rent. It is okay to dream.
Telling you this, I am more American. Low tide sucks
bare the land at our feet. The dike served only to keep
salt out. We thank the traffic on I-5 for being light,
thank the frogs for returning to the algae-green ponds.
Try to have faith in reclamation. The far-off house that
hovers serene above the water makes it possible to
imagine: a glass bowl filled with apples, the scent of
coffee, my hand slipping around your waist as the trees
behind us gloom on. It's the Medicine Creek treaty, this
land bought for less than the down payment on a rambler,
the U.S. Fish and Wildlife Service, the waterfowl hunt,
the barns we passed so white. Empty though never
derelict, as if their scale made them gods. You are right,
there is no way we could afford the insurance or
groceries. We couldn't even lease a car. Think of the
dark water under our feet, the military base we drove
past. Life would be impossible. We would be bound to
this place by rush hour. But it is so beautiful. Where
else would we go? It's the river that runs from the
mountain, years of improper sediment distribution, the
plight of the salmon, the receding glaciers. My father's
climbing days are behind him. But did you want to?
Yes. Never. Always. Everything has a cost: the dream
of here, the sun dipping behind Anderson Island, the
slim tributaries, the fizz of the tide refilling the delta.

He Is Risen

Great-grandfather spits the earth
from his mouth. He asks for his teeth,
asks for vodka and sputters the only sermon
he knows – *No, it was never the axe*
but the whispering saw that thrilled me.
He speaks of the valley's pre-dam rivers, so thick
with fish he thought they were running silver,
of time before pylons and power stations
when houses were lit from within.

Ghost River

I   Aquifer *n*.: a sung prayer which uses liturgical text by the Italian
Dominican theologian and philosopher Thomas Aquinas.[1]

What is faith
if not the belief
in water
we cannot see?

*

We drink from the hosepipe
a mouthful of darkness.

So that's what the centre
of the earth tastes like.

II   Aquifer *n*.: a subterranean repository.[2]

Beneath the homestead
of my ancestors,
the time-blackened sauna
and fruit trees,
the apartment complexes
and strip malls,
the DMV
and high school,
beneath the K-Mart

---

[1] The critical piece of this plan is the development of an aquifer protection steering committee.

[2] Due to the shallow nature of this geologic unit, the District proposed the development of an aquifer protection plan which would define the aquifer boundaries and allow the District to affect management strategies to protect the integrity of the existing water quality and quantity parameters of this valuable resource.

and the Walmart,
Valley Highway
and Dairy Queen,
beneath the cornfields
and the lettuce,
cabbages and broccoli,
beneath the fertiliser, pesticides,
cattle pens and milk barn,
beneath salal and Douglas fir,
cedar and mycelium,
kissing the underbelly
of Big Soos and Sawyer,
there are ghost rivers
from which we all drink.

There is deeper water yet.

III   Aquifer *v.*: to repress or withhold.[3]

She will not drink.
She dreams black water.

    *

Imagine a glass:
half empty
half

    *

What is data that deals in thirst?
Whose currency is water?

---

[3] Figure 3.4 shows the precipitation trends over the period 1945 to 1995. The graph indicates the area has experienced relative drought conditions since 1984.

IV   Aquifer *n.*: the malign shadow that sometimes appears in scans.[4]

We are told that our hearts should be glad,
palm to palm with black water, she prays.
Holy, holy, holy.

*

What shall I call her?
Grandmother? Ghost River?

*

Ghost River? Grandmother?
Is it you I taste in this glass?

V   Aquifer *v.*: to gather the unconsolidated possessions of the deceased.[5]

What remains are gloves, cut glass necklaces,
handkerchiefs, a clock, pantyhose.

VI   Aquifer *n.*: the small font at the entrance or exit of a church.[6]

She said: *Come.*
Each unconsolidated
sediment is welcome here.

The sediments came
and fell upon their knees
to wash her feet.

---

[4] The idealised upward sequence for a single, nonglacial/glacial cycle is fine-grained fluvial sediments, coarse-grained sand and gravel glacial advance outwash, glacial till, and coarse-grained recessional outwash deposits. The sequence can be complicated by potential pro- and post-glacial lake deposits. The ideal sequence is rarely seen.

[5] It is generally accepted that four or more glaciations have occurred in the Puget Lowland during the Pleistocene. Each of the glacial episodes and the intervening non-glacial periods left unconsolidated sediments in the area.

[6] The extent of the aquifer was not known at the beginning of the project.

Blue

This is a colour. No,
this is a family.
I say wavelength, nanometre,
terahertz and this becomes science
the way blood turns family
to DNA.

I have never known
the meaning of blue-blooded –
only that we are not – but I know the veins
of my arms and the fat blue veining
of my mother's legs. Hereditary,
she told me. She makes a map

of our rivers: Columbia,
Chehalis, Nisqually, Skagit,
Snohomish, Duwamish, Stillaguamish,
Snoqualmie. Snoqualmie,
a town I was raised in
split by a river. No, the river was not

blue. This is the mistaken identity
of water. The river was mountain run-off,
sedimentary leak, log jams
and algae. Who knew
anything could set down roots
in water so quick?

My step-brothers jump
from the trestle bridge,
their legs testing
just how deep the river
sinks. I fall
a lesser distance

and learn the meaning
of black and blue.
Not ultramarine or cobalt,
Prussian or Morton Salt –
this is nothing synthetic,
this is blood.

Home is a matter of paint on walls.
I ask for sky blue.
I do not know that sky
is not a colour,
but a display of physics –
a Rayleigh scattering.

Outside the room with sky walls
two hyacinths grow.
I must have looked the part of blue girl
to those boys who brought them
to my door. Funeral flowers,
my father calls them.

I learn the names of flowers:
iris, anemone, cornflower, harebell,
globe thistle, delphinium.
I am taught the names
of stones: azurite,
lapis lazuli.

My mother with blue eyes
is to me what the Madonna
draped in blue robes
is to a world of guilty Catholics.
She keeps grandma's ice blue
rosary on the bedside table.

There are other names
for this: cyan, robin's egg,
powder, crevasse.
But none comes close
to the cold of those stones
in her fingers.

I did not get her eyes
but her hands and feet.
And it is her voice I carry
somewhere beyond memory.
It is her voice I think of
when I think of grace.

PASSAGE

Between 1791 and 1795, British naval officer, Captain George Vancouver commanded HMS *Discovery* on an expedition to North America's Pacific coast, exploring what is now Alaska, British Columbia, Washington, Oregon and California, and producing charts of the region's complex waterways. Based on his discoveries, he asserted that an internal watercourse linking the Pacific and Atlantic Oceans, the illusive Northwest Passage, did not exist.

Having fallen out of favour with the Royal Society and in poor health, Vancouver struggled to complete the manuscript of his voyage. He died in 1798, age forty. *A Voyage of Discovery to the North Pacific Ocean, and Round the World* was published posthumously by his brother. The maps Vancouver created of America's North Pacific coast continued to serve as guides well into the modern day. The many names he ascribed to the region's geo-graphic features and waterways remain.

'And when the writer alleges, that from the age of thirteen, his whole life, to the commencement of this expedition, (fifteen months only excepted) has been devoted to constant employment in His Majesty's naval service, he feels, and with all possible humility, that he has some claims to the indulgence of a generous public; who, under such circumstances, will not expect to find elegance of direction, purity of style, or unexceptionable grammatical accuracy: but will be satisfied with 'a plain unvarnished' relation, given with a rigid attention to the truth of such transactions and circumstances as appeared to be worthy of recording by a naval officer, whose greatest pride is to deserve the appellation of being zealous in the service of his king and country.'

GEORGE VANCOUVER

Theoretical Geographers

A slow leak is filling George Vancouver's left boot.
Rain. Impenetrable, unnavigable, endless
rain. Among his men the pretended discoveries
of De Fuca and De Fonte have been revived.
He retires to his cabin. Childhood, Kings Lynn.
In this wooden room all he can see
has been discovered. Nothing left
but to exist in the bleak small space
that knowing creates. Theoretical geographers
and their Northwest Passage nonsense.
Not a whiff of estuary on the wind.
What of his laborious and enterprising
exertions? Pulled from history
with one inglorious suck. De Fuca,
De Fonte. The tedious knock
against the hull.

V is for Vancouver

George coughs twice and begins.
> *Valiant Vancouver*
> *Visionary Vancouver*
> *Valorous Vancouver*
> *Venerated Vancouver*
> *Virile Vancouver*

Oh, not again.
> *A Naval Officer lives*
> *to serve the Crown.*
> *A Naval Officer lives*
> *to serve to the Crown.*

But the blood has found
its way to the planted seed.
George restores his
mirror to the bureau.
What did he know of *amor*
save virgin territory was a myth?
And intercourse? Friendly exchange
or the communication of inlets
and the continent's interior waters.
Virtuous Vancouver slides
his sabre into its scabbard
and vanquishes his curiosity
about the animal within.

The principled process of deduction

George Vancouver is pleased to be momentarily
overcome by the quandary posed
by the erect poles of New Dungeness.
So evenly placed, so very tall
and straight, and with such might
and substance. How noble it is to be sated
by the principled process of deduction.
Not once has he mused upon
the woman's thighs
emergent from the water.
Venus was never so radiantly-torsoed!
How easily a man of lesser nature
might succumb to enticement,
imagining her delighted fingers
brushing the split mouth of a clam.

Church

No church in this land, just the dull green spire
of the forest and, somewhere beyond,
the haloed crags. George Vancouver stands on deck
picking pye from his teeth. He's not thinking
about God, though he worries his men
have forgotten who to pray to. No –
he's thinking about trees.
Their impossible tallness, their beautiful utility.
What keels they could be, what masts!
To take an axe to the damp and abundant trunks,
to seize the base of a tree in his fist
and strip it of branches, to thrust it like a spear
into the black obsequious water,
to whittle it to a needle
and prod his wretched teeth.
Outward, outward the trees unfold,
the new wood so white he can hardly see.

Vancouver, dreaming

George sees himself birthed
from the bald head
of an eagle. The eagle
bears his face, the mountains,
the water, the resplendent trees.
His heart beats for a star
not yet named –
a star as white as feathers
and sewn by his hands.

Pseudotsuga menziesii

Even as the sun cuts through impenetrable
cloud to illuminate the white wig
of George Vancouver, my attention
is on the man in the undergrowth:
the man becoming tree.
To rest my hand on his back
and feel the vigour of his inhalation
is to know the sweetness
of pitch, its golden ooze,
crystalline honey. Black hills
plunging to black water. I confuse
his pulse with the forest's heart.
I tell him to empty his pockets,
cloth is a poor shroud for the seed.
He asks if I know the saying
not every man is a puzzle,
but every puzzle is a man.
Black hills, black hills
beyond black hills.
He tells me it is not theft
to take what is freely given –
find a man who did not envy the crane
that strode with lordly step
over the land without a possessor.

Kulshan

George Vancouver lifts his face to the sun.
The weather is fine, his cock is hard.
Hard for the very land from which his men
gather roses, gooseberries, and rest
sea-wearied bodies on luxuriant grasses.
No Eve to scupper their conquest
of this pleasure ground,
no raging God to throw them out.
This shall be his and this shall be his.
With Adamic candour he titles
the presiding mountain
after third lieutenant Baker.
But there is brimstone
in the bead of magma
beneath its white and placid dome.
He dreams a cold hand
over his mouth.

Rainier

What other proof could there be
of God's remoteness
than this mountain
so breathlessly high,
so pristine in its frigid garment?
Not even in his most fevered dream
had George Vancouver
envisaged a peak so void
of earthly substance.
For days it had been
on his periphery,
mistaken for cloud.
But with what glory
it holds aloft its name,
and how relentlessly
does each inlet and tributary
pull in its direction
that were it not
for the sheerness of the banks,
the black mass of trees,
George might be hoisted
atop that God-seat
which, in its perfect
uselessness, confounds.

Having considered with impartiality the excellencies & deficiencies of the land

George Vancouver observes the calmness
of the water, how graciously it parts.
So welcoming has this country been
that he finds himself seized
by visions of subtle improvements.
How quickly his men could disencumber
the forests of their undergrowth.
And in that black loam, newly cleared
and fortified by his ingenuity,
what a range of esculents, fruit trees
and nutritious exotics he might sow.
Despite his huntsmen failing
to land any aquatic varieties,
the feathered tribe is of an entirely
agreeable character. And with such a glut
of succulent beasts, he can see no need
to retain the skunk, whose effluvia
render coexistence intolerable.

The burial rituals of the inhabitants

What did he think
of the bodies of children
held aloft in baskets,
bodies on the beaches,
bodies in canoes
suspended between trees,
the feeling of having
entered a church
after the service had begun?
If George Vancouver
was unsettled
by the wind in the trees,
the wind his men
mistook for rattlesnakes,
he did not show it.
It was the silence
that followed.
The emptiness
lay over the ship
for hours until lifted
by the exhausted
breath of a seal.

In the name of, and for, His Britannic Majesty, His Heirs and successors

George Vancouver dreams his death
as an anchor. Down, down.
No time to measure the depth,
only mouthful after mouthful of salt.
He wakes, his stomach turned.
Not even the pleasant breezes
springing up can right it.
Too much grog or a bad mussel.
At low tide their black eyes
clustered on the rocks. Inside,
they were small and wrinkled ears.
What of the other beasts
that heard his proclamation?
A loathsome torment
stalks the bank. There is darkness
at the base of the trees. He would speak
but for the weight on his tongue.

Small Distances

Tell me you cared for the deer
sanguine in the fields, the roses
you approached with such
considerable forwardness.
Tell me you would have bid
farewell to the *Discovery*.
I see you with a scattering
of children harvesting
geoducks and salmon berries
in the shadow of the firs.
Pity they called you back, George.
There are lives that demand
nothing from the moon but light.

Passage

George, didn't your knees get sore
praying for mercy and fresh water?
I am sore from the hands
that could not right the ship inside me.
If you knew anything about birth,
you would know the passage
I sought was not so different.
Far from motherhood's bright shore
I held my breath and waited
for you to arrive and give name
to something. Who can I blame?
I drown again and again.

The death of George Vancouver

No fanfare when history slipped
you into St Peter's churchyard
among the lesser Lords and bakers
and the cousins of unknown poets.
Didn't you miss England's geometry
of lawns and walls, of rooftops
and steeples? Better the slow
decline than death by duel.
Better dirt than water.
No need to sink your head
against my chest and wallow.
There is England: Richmond Hill's
attempt at elevation, the lawn
so green, so perfect
and green. Praise its utter
sameness. Praise its fields
of grass. Praise the land
coming into vision: a strip
of green light hovering.

In the *Discovery* sloop of war

My daughter plays in the next room.
She is learning possessives: my hands,
your hands. It was only a handful
of days ago that I was writing your death.
She asks her father to lift her to the window. *Up, up!*
That you never had children made it more final.
Today, I am thinking of beginnings.
The gentle breeze that dawn you sailed
out of Carrack road, the articles you acquired
for your long exile to places remote
and barbarous: portable broth and sour-krout,
malt and hops, wheat, yeast, seed mustard,
the surgeon's rob of oranges and lemons.
I think of the ceramic urn under my sister's desk,
her luminous kimchi and too-salty asparagus.
The walls of her shed are lined
with preparations for a coming storm.
George, spare me the disappointment
I know is coming (the fruit and vegetables
indifferent and exceedingly expensive, the good beef
too soon exhausted), spare me the loss
of an anchor when no other can be procured.

I dream I am held

Sometimes I dream I am held in my mother's arms
or the salmon are returning or it is March and the fields
of Mt Vernon are white with snow geese.

But the geese take flight as soon as I arrive
and the salmon, though they scale ladder after ladder,
never reach home and I wake, as ever, alone.

George Vancouver, you are not my father

but if you were, I would ask you
where you were when I needed help
with geography homework and why
you never attended any of my softball games.
George, I am America's daughter. I dream
of mountains, of forests thick as fog.
George, I am raising a daughter
whose imagination will be shaped
by low hills, stone churches,
cold wind off the North Sea.
George, you are not her father.
You are not the father of my nation,
though where would I be without you?
Everywhere I once was, you are, forever.

Indivisible

Though I once lived on the land
that I now see from your ship,
time has removed me
the way the trees diminished in beauty
until they became invisible
as the men you sought to immortalise.
No man is a mountain.
Even home is too simple a name
for that cradle of rock.
Were you so afraid of being forgotten?
It's time to let go, George.
Glaciers melt and rise
as bubbles across the mudflats,
trees become the land.

Myth

A woman rose from the earth;
a woman gave birth to a mountain
or a walrus or an eel; a woman
with a sheep's head terrorised
the dreams of young men;
a woman shed her feet
and grew two black hooves;
a woman made love to a bear
or a goat or a stallion;
a woman shat a stone
that would become Pangea;
a woman's sharp tongue
turned into a beak; a woman
suckled a pig or a lynx
or a monkey; a woman woke
to find her sex was a rose;
a woman hovered serene
on a gaping bivalve and a man
reached out to help her down.
Do you know the purpose of a shell?
she asked, batting her eyelashes
like two cedar branches.

We Have Kissed the Four-legged Gods Goodnight

after Enclave (ii) by Tamsin Nagel

There a dainty hoof points from around the trunk,
a wing, bristled wolf pelt, boar tusk,
udders, tail, round ear, pointed ear,
fur, feathers and the neck of a doe –
incomplete gestures laid down among the snags.
Hear no pulse, grunt, growl, scratch,
howl, groan – not even a leaf to rustle.
See no breath curl from nostrils
or heaving ribs. No steam
rises from the furrows.

And where is the moon (saviour,
guardian, protector,
companion?) that was made
to watch over them:
on the altar beside the candlesticks
and flowers, incense and bells,
in a box made from maple
and padlocked with solid brass (the key
is in the reverend's pocket).
It is rumoured her heart is still beating.

None of us is where we ought to be

Not this auk, racoon, lynx, beaver, fulmar, grey wolf or bison.
It is not out of morbid curiosity – though I would like to know

who fired the felling shot and what happened to their eyes, hearts,
lungs and bellies that would have been full on flesh or grass

(are they preserved in canopic jars as offerings to some other gods?
Or were they left to the crows or ground for dog food?) –

but because through them I've learned
to mourn our shared losses, that each day I return

to sit on this bench or walk among them, reading
the given names: *Canis lupis, Fulmar glacialis,*

Castor canadensis, Sturnus vulgaris, Panthera tigris.
I carry this language strange on my tongue

and wear their death-pelts. And when I come home
and beg you to make love to me (your words, not mine) –

what I really want is to have these furs and feathers
taken off my shoulders; the hooves, beaks, claws and horns

removed from my side; have all use of language
stripped from my mouth. Help me forget

the red deer fawn and the *Ovis aries* taken from their mothers
by joining me in this one act of creation.

Lunar Distances

You have been measuring the distance between your bed and the voice of Eric Sloan, the makeshift babysitter who sang as he sat vigil at your bedside. Your bed and the long apartment corridor your dad walks down.

In order for your measurements to be accurate, you must provide the raw data and use the correct formula.

But you cannot now distinguish Eric's voice from Neil Young's or your own. You remember the lyrics: *come a little bit closer / hear what I have to say.* You remember pretending to be asleep.

In the dream you unpack the matryoshka dolls to discover the smallest is a moon. The distance between the first doll and the moon is a figure that only makes sense in the dream.

You lay on your back and the moon presses against your spine. The midwife runs the cold measuring tape over your belly. She frowns.

You measure the distance from the pillow wedged beneath you to night in the playground, your corduroy dress riding up your thighs as you swing across the monkey bars, the lunar eclipse behind you. You bring your hands to your face expecting that metallic tang.

The Board of Longitude writes to inform you that your measurements are incorrect. Lunar measurements require the utmost precision.

You measure the distance between your headboard and moonrise over the Cascades. Between summer on Sourdough Mountain and the moon-blind stars.

The grey marks on the moon's face are not craters but stretch marks. These could have been avoided with a strict moisturising regimen and abiding by the measurements.

A letter arrives from the Astronomer Royal: 'In agreement with The Board of Longitude, I assert that the instruments do not give false measurements.'

You measure the distance between your convex navel and the moon as it passes from the neighbour's rooftop to your kitchen window. You tangle yourself in white tape. Bound like a mummy, you rest on the kitchen floor.

Imagine a mirror where the moon is one side of the reflection and your baby is the other.

With her hands on you, the specialist says, 'It (the moon) appears to have deviated manifestly from the truth.'

Corona

Her birth is light or so I tell myself
as I am wheeled from bright room
to bright room. Only here it is brighter
because this is the room in which she
is being born. Light because for days
there has been no sleep.
Light because she is cradled
in my body like flame
in a kerosene lamp.
Light does not want to be alone.
It seeks out dying stars, televisions,
even this fluorescent room
of masked faces.
I was told that for her coronation
she would wear my body
as a crown and I would know
the white pain of light.
Corona because what else
can light wear.
But she is not crowning.
Instead, she is rising.
Her body lifted, backlit
by LEDs. Her body glorious
and blazing. Her body
rising as the sun must.

Cottonwood

In 1937 the sisters of Mary Mother of Grace planted an avenue of cottonwoods so those among them who had never seen snow could imagine what it might be like.

My daughter rests her hand against the trunk. The tree is bare; the buds are months away.

The woods were off limits to us as children. Our parents made certain we understood that they belonged to someone else.

The sisters sit in the shade of the cottonwood. Some read their bibles in silence. Some embroider cloth of fine white cotton.

In the beginning was the word, and the word was with wood, and the word was wood.

It was snowing that day we drove to the hospital to learn about birth. What could prepare us for the endless corridors, the white cotton bedding, the small plastic cribs?

Language replaces language replaces trees.

Nothing could prepare us for the amazement of green after days of white cotton.

We were children mystified by summer snow.

The Time of Lace

After her birth, we entered the time of lace. Everything too fragile, everything adorned: lichen on boulders, wild garlic in the dene, names carved in stone.

When I was not much older than she is now, my mother took me to see the lace makers. I remember a series of rooms, the voices of elderly women. Lace gives shape to absence.

Beauty is labour. The hard work of birth, piped white icing on a birthday cake, the tiresome movements of the dressmaker's hand, the energy it takes to flower. Christening gown, lace gloves, cow parsley, meadowsweet.

There was a vintage lace dress at the thrift store that I admired but never bought for fear of damaging it. Motherhood is about the metallic bite of the zipper, the brittle lace.

From under the bed, I pull my wedding dress, our daughter's white broderie anglaise dress. Time falls through us. It opens us. Outside, the caterpillars and snails make lacework of the kale, the marjoram, the hydrangea.

The pillow covers we sleep on arrived in a box addressed in my grandmother's lacy penmanship. I run my fingers over the bright embroidered flowers, the many questions I forgot to ask her becoming lace.

American Mustard

It is English summer, the shock–yellow
fields take me back to the car
parked on the gravel shoulder,
dry heat and fields I believed
were mustard because they were yellow,
because my father told me so.
A line of yellow mustard becomes
the centre line of a highway,
a thread pulled from the hem
of my mother's dress,
the trim on an Easter bonnet,
a fat ribbon of heart ache.
I believed the apples
that blushed the flat plains
of the Yakima no different
from that which Eve held.
I believed we were of that land.
Belief becomes memory
becomes myth becomes
mustard: the scent of grief,
my grandmother's voice,
the answer I have
no question for.

Cast of an Irish Deer

This is how I imagine death will arrive,
without cloak or flesh to cover
vertebrae – the blank space
between finger-thin ribs
clear demarcation of other from living.

Not the white one would expect
of bone, but cast from an oily, unknown ore,
he towers on four femurs
no bigger than my wrists. Of course
his cloven hooves are pointed.

Long palmed and clawed,
his antlers float as a veil
blown back by wind.
The sleek scythe of his jaw
laughs with hunger, eyeless sockets
say there is no need for sight
where I am going.

As ash falls on my mother's garden

a city is submerged, another learns
the friability of houses, sea walls.

Here, nothing can stop the rapture,
the second coming of the forests.

Does the ash know its origins?
There are centuries falling

on my mother's garden. Time covers
the porch, the hollyhocks and hostas.

There is time in the grass,
on the inconsequential pavement.

She can wear a tree, a forest
on her fingertip. What is gone is gone.

To hold the world in our palms
and settle the dust

we must hold our grief
as a plum its stone.

Tahoma

Up from the river valley,
the yawn of farmland,

second growth, moss-laid floor
and the trunks of cedar;

from salmonberry, huckleberry,
neon yellow lichen and the orange boom

of mushroom; beyond spruce
and fir stunted by altitude

to heather tufts and stone outcrops
far above the tree line;

a mile off, across the moraine
the mountain rests on its haunches,

grey and summer-thinned
beneath feathered glaciers.

The mountain goats know
this is all and enough.

What you hold

Removing the honeydew melon from the bowl, I find myself in awe of the fine hairs that grow near its stem, hairs blonde and short like those on the backs of my fingers. So many days I find myself newborn. Holding this melon or looking up to swallows in the back alley or the way I can fall into a marigold. Do I believe in wasted time? Time spent watching bees, stirring onions, those silent hours when my daughter slept on my chest and all I could do was listen. Across the road, a woman's husband is dying. Carers come and go. I watch for them as if they were the measure of time. This morning as I was writing, I paused to watch a spider climb the white wall in front of me. Was I not that spider once, learning the lessons of vertical space: love the air, trust what you hold.

Northwest Passage

My sister places a handful of my grandmother's ashes in a cedar box. On the box are horses. She dreams of horses, dreams of grandmother opening the box the way flames open a roof. I have seen trees erupt with manes of fire. I have seen hillsides gallop towards rivers.

*

Stay a while. I would like us to ride horses the way I imagine my grandmother rode through the young valley. There are no freeways, no car lots. The drive-in is coming but a long way off. If there is only one fence, it is easier to jump.

*

Picture my grandmother as a horse, a horse without a rider, a horse black as her hair, black as the fossil in the spare room unearthed as they blasted the hills to make way for the interstate. The smell of dynamite is in the air and at the mouth of the tunnel she gallops through.

*

If I am using you to delay the grief that I know is coming, what happens when we part? Imagine us cresting Chinook Pass to greet the dry breeze of Yakima County. The dark forests roll until dissolved by sage. Beyond the sage, juniper. Beyond the juniper, grasses. And somewhere beyond the grasses, mountains and rivers and forests and mountains and rivers and...

*

America is nothing if not longing. The valley a riparian marsh uninterrupted by the cornfields, the river snaking loose through cattails, the call of the redwing blackbird, the unwritten name of *Oemleria cerasiformis*. Too far back. Knowledge erases itself the way a tree may burn from the inside leaving nothing more than a hollow trunk.

*

I no longer know if I set out to write about arrivals or departures or why I assumed there was any difference. It doesn't matter if the clouds we kick up are dust or ash or if it is with you that I ride or if I am seated behind my grandmother in the old Ford and we are driving to where they drove the final spike of the transcontinental railroad. I see a bald field, and in the distance, two tracks merging.

Tectonics

The argument had something
to do with tectonic plates,
the way they moved and how,
but so much time spent
working from memory means
I have forgotten the point
and the subduction zone
now has no name but exists
as dropping off point
not far from where I may
have looked once when waking
to sea stacks crowned with mist
and waves beating the shore
or here now at the front gate
of a small brick nursery.
A number of years ago,
I watched two children
put together a puzzle.
I held one piece uncertain
of when it became so difficult.
If all new thinking is about loss
perhaps that is why these
part-memories return as I let go
of her hand. Our days together
belonging now in a past
that until yesterday
was the present.
I used to believe the purpose
of life was movement.
I crossed oceans, continents.
I never stopped to consider
the mountain's stillness
only its power:
old earth rising as new.

Gather

Start with the water beneath the roses or the water
your daughter wades in or rain on the nasturtiums
or the clear water of the Teanaway or the water held
in bodies or in the bath house where you learned
the intimacy of female space.
Gather it in strands and hold it loosely
the way you might hold your daughter's hair.
Braiding water is easier if you close your eyes.
Gather the North Sea cold around your waist,
steam on thighs and pubic hair,
the receding waterline of Lake Cle Elum
and the pool your grandmother swims
warmed by a sun that does not set
and her body forever in motion.

NOTES

Ghost River (24)
The text in the footnotes is from the 'King County Water District 111 North Meridian Aquifer Protection Plan' (March 1996).

Passage (32)
The sequence incorporates and adapts words and phrases from *A Voyage of Discovery to the North Pacific Ocean, and Round the World*, vols. 1 & 2, London: G.G. and J. Robinson, Paternoster-Row, and J. Edwards, Pall-Mall, 1798, and *Menzies' Diary of Vancouver's Voyage: April to October*, 1792, ed. C.F. Newcombe, M.D., Victoria: William H. Cullin, 1923.

Lunar Distances (58)
This poem incorporates and adapts words and phrases from an academic paper by Nicholas A. Doe, 'Captain Vancouver's longitudes, 1792', *Journal of Navigation*, 48(3), pp.374-88, September 1995.

Tectonics (70)
This poem references a line from Robert Hass's, 'Meditation at Lagunitas': 'All the new thinking is about loss.'